D1426984

touch the feet

by Frieda McRae

touch the feet

By Frieda McRae

Copyright © 2008 Frieda McRae

ISBN 978-81-906277-1-9

Published by

MOUNTAIN PEAK

Mountain Peak
Kanu Chambers, C-2 Sanwal Nagar,
New Delhi - 110049
office@mountainpeak.biz

Scriptures quoted are from the *Good News Bible* © 1994 published by the Bible Societies/ HarperCollins Publishers Ltd., *UK Good News Bible* © American Bible Society 1966, 1971, 1976, 1992. Used with permission.

*Printed at Devtech Publishers and Printers Pvt. Ltd.,
Email: devtech_printers@sify.com*

Producing this book has been a lifetime desire... and thanks to Chris Hale and Peter Hicks, who were willing to believe in me, the music album has happened. Thanks to my children: Sonu, Lindsay, Kirti, Luke, Asher, Sheva and Nibha; all were truly supportive, pushing me on when I hesitated, and lifting me up when I was down. Words cannot express my thanks for the love and encouragement my husband Ken gave continually - always seeing the project as important. Thanks to Elizabeth Lal for being ready for 'anything' in order to make it happen, and to the community in Sailakui, who were faithful in their encouragement. Grateful thanks to Angelika, whose financial help kept the project alive. And finally, heartfelt thanks to the Great Music Director of my life, Jesus, without whom, none of this would have had a reason to happen.

Thanks also, to those people who worked relentlessly on editing and re-editing and re-editing the re-editing (no-kidding); thanks to Ros Bunney, Willi Barton, and especially Marvin Landis, my brother-in-law, who taught me how to write, persevering to the end, enduring patiently my lack of skills, until I came up with something worth reading. Thanks!

And a final thanks to Shalom, who turned the book into a graphic delight. ❧

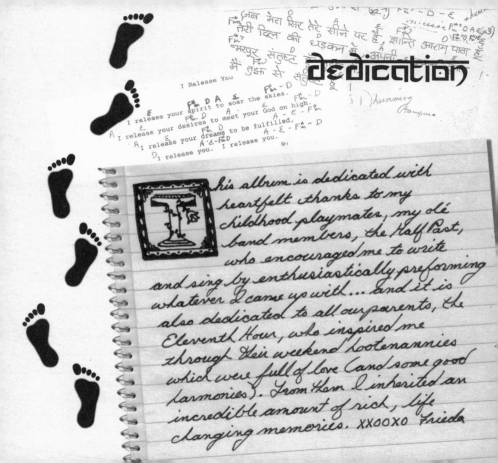

जब मेरा सिर तेरे सीने पर है
तेरी दिल की धड़कन
भरपूर संतुष्ट अपनी
मैं तुझ से स...

dedication

I Release You

I release your spirit to soar the skies.
I release your desires to meet your God on high.
I release your dreams to be fulfilled,
I release you.   I release you.

T his album is dedicated with
heartfelt thanks to my
childhood playmates, my olé
band members, the Half Past,
who encouraged me to write
and sing by enthusiastically preforming
whatever I came up with... and it is
also dedicated to all our parents, the
Eleventh Hour, who inspired me
through their weekend "hootenannies"
which were full of love (and some good
harmonies). From them I inherited an
incredible amount of rich, life
changing memories. xxooxo Frieda

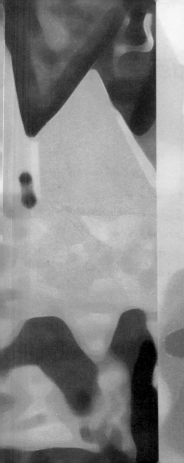

introduction

In 1974 we were hippies—world travellers, roaming about in the "mystical" Far East. Straying off the normal path of drugs and meditation, we found ourselves in an orphanage looking after one hundred children; our self-absorbed happy-hippy lives were turned upside down as we walked into a realm of life we had never dared to imagine – the realm of God. It was a great, nearly unbelievable discovery. We found no hidden path to paradise, no steep climb up a spiritual mountain to attain immortality. There was just "God"… and one hundred children. One hundred grubby hands and feet and a sinner's guilty conscience proved to be a recipe for revelation – the revelation of a God who taught us how to touch the dirty, dusty feet.

Sharing life experiences in an understandable way has not always been easy. After sharing at a women's meeting in England, I learned that the women had asked my hostess if what I had said was actually true! It is because of the truth that I share the events which turned my life around.

Tragedy during my teenage years had the potential to negatively affect my future, and that process had begun. India became a "last resort" in a search to find a reason to live. Because the journey to India was a search for truth – a search for God, I have often been asked, "and did you find God?" It is usually asked sceptically, without any expectancy of a positive reply… for knowing God is an arrogant claim! Would the "mystical" quest of seeking God be more attractive, more acceptable, and more humble if God remained unfound?

The following account ends at a beginning, for more than thirty years have passed since my husband and I first arrived in India and established a children's home which has been functioning for nearly the same amount of time. The inspiration for this book came from the poor, the outcasts, and the many dirty little feet that touched our lives. During our early years, when we first began taking in children, we lived like nomads; no one wanted to rent a house to our large, expanding family. We finally managed to buy a piece of land and moved on to it with more than fifty boys, but immediately ran into trouble – no water. The nearby well which we had been counting on dried up, and we had to haul our water from as far away as eight kilometres in oil canisters on the back of a bicycle every day. Every drop was counted, and every spilled drop was grieved over. Indian summers are hot; creating thirst that is nearly unquenchable. We had to do something – fast.

We dug a well – a deep well, which provided an abundance of good, clean water. Sweat and tears accompanied us as we established our children's home. It is difficult to explain all that we went through, and this narrative barely touches our beginnings. Our land, which had been a dry riverbed, turned into a thriving community of families, fields to harvest, and orchards. Had we not found God, this never would have happened. Our sweat and tears were turned into wine, like Jesus turned the water into wine to make his friends happy; we too were given gifts we did not deserve. My songs were not inspired by the hard work or the spilled water; it was the wine, the "living water" that we discovered when we dug very, very deep.

In 1974, while desperately trying to quench our thirst for truth, we were

unaware that God had prepared chilled glasses for us, ready to be filled. We had no idea that the dusty, rocky earth we were walking on was holy ground, and that we were about to meet the one who loves us more than his life. Just as Jesus told the woman who had offered him a drink of water drawn from a well:

"… 'If only you knew what God gives and who it is that is asking you for a drink, you would ask him, and he would give you life-giving water.'"
John 4:10 ❧

9

touch the feet
for you are made from dust
and you know that the one who
has his throne on

so ... touch the feet.

i touch the feet
i feel the flesh of him
whose tears and blood are mixed
to become wine for me

through his sweat .... i touch his feet.

touch the feet of the Christ
wipe the stain from him who died
standing up unashamed
stripped of pride it remains, to

touch the feet
touch the feet
touch the feet
touch the feet

पर छुओ धूल से बने तू और जब जानो वह

जो धूल में चला, पैर छुओ धूल से बने हो

Black crescent-shaped eyes peeped out from behind half-veiled faces. Thick black eyebrows and handlebar moustaches provided a frame for beautifully sculpted features. Silver and gold adorned the women, decorating their ears, noses, necks, wrists, and ankles. Even the poor were ornamented as queens and kings, boldly wearing all of their wealth as the only safe place to keep it. Women proudly displayed their beautiful black braided hair, or hair twisted high into a peak at the back of their heads… a luxury unknown to Western women. It was no wonder that heads turned to stare as I walked down their streets; they were amazed at the "plainness" of the Western woman. I wore wooden earrings and a very old green baggy dress that could have been my grandmother's. Nothing could compare to the elegant five meters of seamless cloth wrapped around their bodies, tucked and folded, without a pin or button to hold it together… the sari, one of India's wonders, and India, a land which seemed to have been birthed from a story book, exploded in reality before my very eyes.

Cows stood stock-still or even lay down to sleep in the centre of New Delhi streets. Pigs scurried out of alleyways, running in front of bicycles and vehicles, causing havoc, but unstopped in their mission. The poor, the rich, the educated, the illiterate, the sick, the crazy… all share the same city, the same streets, and enjoy the same tastes. The children I had dreamt of, the children who had lured me to India, were also there, lining the streets with their begging bowls and imploring eyes.

Thousands of miles away from anything familiar, I was overwhelmed with

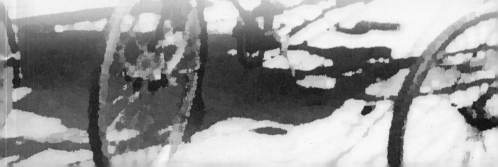

discovery, and felt a strange calm that comes with a great sigh of relief and the peace of finally reaching "home." Home! What an unlikely place to arrive at and feel so at home! What a strange feeling… what did it mean? In 1974, I was twenty years old and had just travelled half way around the world to reach my destination… India! Who would have guessed that out of my dreams reality would appear?

A single day in New Delhi was enough, I was in a rush to put all my energy into volunteering in a children's home. Travelling straight north, towards the Himalayas, I arrived in the mountain town of Mussoorie on the doorstep of some conservatively dressed people who began to scrutinize me, casually socializing with me while handing out tea and biscuits. They nodded knowingly to each other and in hushed tones, discussed what to do with a volunteer whom they had not expected, and who obviously, did not meet their expectations. Sadly, I realized that the children's home was still far away.

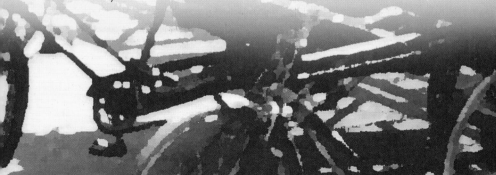

"Expected!" They had no clue that I was coming! Before coming I had written to the founder of the home, introducing myself, and received her warm reply, gladly accepting my offer. The home's board members had been "kept in the dark", which seemed to be working to my advantage, for at least I was here. Had they been given the chance to respond the reply might have been negative. My appearance at their home created a problem for them, and now they needed to find a solution. The founder (who looked to be about ninety years old going on a hundred and twenty) lived at the children's home and was lovingly known by all as *Dadiji* (Grandmother). Although she herself was often "kept in the dark" about what was going on around her, she was highly respected and greatly loved. The only agreement they could reach was that a decision would have to be made later during a "proper" board meeting, which gave me time to study them more closely.

They were very unusual (weird?) people, and yet extremely nice, which made me wonder at the enmity I felt towards them. I had never encountered this sort of Christ-follower before. They were my very strange enemy indeed – driving Land Rovers, singing ancient hymns from moth-eaten hymnbooks, their medical team performing major surgery on wooden benches in remote villages, and smiling – constantly. There was certainly a difficult future ahead of me if I were to remain in their midst. There was a time in my childhood when our grandmother looked after my sisters and me for three weeks. I smiled so much for Grandma that my cheeks got sore. Behind Dadiji's kind smile was great wisdom, which made the wrinkles that framed her face add another dimension to what she saw when she looked at you. One could only respond to her smile with truth.

When my father realized I had purchased a ticket for India, he was rightfully worried - worried about my attitude to save the world… or at least the orphans. The determination he saw in my eyes caused him to keep all that he would have liked to say bottled up inside. He was defeated, unable to stop the second of his four daughters in her madness. "What in the world does she think she can do by going to India?" It was so visible in his eyes… "Frieda is running away!" He never voiced it out loud, but he thought it. Perhaps it was good that he left it unsaid, for it was evident what I was doing… I was running away and did not want to talk about it. My aim was to run as far away as possible… out of the world would be best. I was running, compelled to run, as though something was urging me onwards. There was no turning back. Our family had been on display for the last five years; it was a chance to be out of view and away from the gossip that idolized our grief. It was time to discover a reason to live.

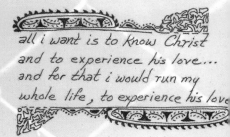

all i want is to know Christ and to experience his love… and for that i would run my whole life, to experience his love

Death had surprised us all. My father, a renowned psychiatrist, was expected to be able to explain everything, but he too, had trouble making sense of life. Day and night continued as always, but life had gone out of control and death immobilized our once happy, fun-loving neighbourhood. Reason to live had been sucked out of us; further hurt seemed impossible, for we were all numb. One thought plagued Dad: had he been home when the murderer entered our house, Mom may not have died, and the mystery of who murdered her may have been solved. Life had been just as hard for him to understand as it was for me. Finding words of wisdom to expound to his four daughters was nearly impossible.

Earlier, when I was still a young child, our father read everything behind the couch; it was where he gained wisdom and revelation. Three couches sat in our front room where he could have sat very comfortably, but he always chose the floor. Bracing himself on his elbows he would lay on his belly between the couch and the wall in the empty space, which formed a walkway to my parents' bedroom. It was a sacred heart spot… behind the couch; I know because I tested it. I went behind the couch to look through my father's magazines, searching for the photographs of needy children. They looked at me with large, longing eyes, as if they were asking me to do something for them. I was a child who had no need; I had parents who loved me, a house, a bed, food, and even a dog. What would it be like to be an orphan? It was hard to imagine no one being there to love you and look out for you. And so, an ambition began to unfold and form in my young spirit.

Plans began to take shape. Money would have to be saved, high school would have to be finished, a plane ticket for India would need to be purchased, and then the orphanage would begin. From then on, there wasn't any more playing "house," instead my playmates were coerced into playing "orphanage," and solemnly promised their allegiance to the orphans in "my orphanage" in India.

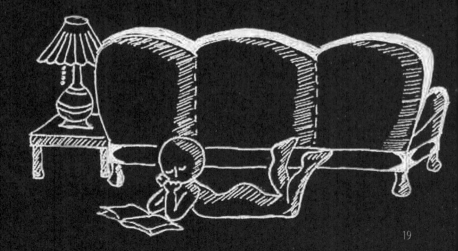

Missionaries often go to poor countries and start orphanages – this raised a big question mark: would I also have to become a missionary? What turns you into a missionary? God? I used to pray to God as though he were my fairy godmother… there to grant my wishes. One of my most fervent prayers was that he would bring my dolly to life. I loved her so much; it seemed the *least* he could do. I even promised God I would not to be taken by surprise when it happened (assuming that the element of surprise would mean weak faith, and I wanted to assure God of my very strong faith). After many tearful prayers, the doll remained a doll.

Realizing that God wasn't going to grant this wish, I drew a little paper god and kept *her* in my pocket… no need for a "holy" and "righteous" God who lived in heaven and threatened us with hell. Paper dolls were understandable and easy to talk to. She was about an inch tall, a real friend with supernatural powers

to help me whenever there was any need. Occasionally, she would be thrown out and a newer, fresher one would replace her. Captive in the control of my imagination, she never let me down. My heart realized that she was not God, but she was an easier form of God to identify with.

Contemplating the possibility of a bigger god led my thoughts to church. Growing up, we had attended a Mennonite church, full of very nice people, but they could never satisfactorily answer my questions concerning God. There were certain people in the church whose faith was "different," if not eccentric, for they believed that Jesus was actually God, and the Bible actually contained the words of God!

For me, the Bible was a book that I had kept on a shelf since fifth grade, when our Sunday School teacher gave us each one of our own. New, shiny, and smooth, it seemed very holy, and indeed, its title was *Holy Bible*. It was reverently kept behind the sliding door at the head of my bed and read only late at night when no one was watching. Its words were unfamiliar… full of kings, wars, faraway lands, and prophets declaring "the word of the Lord!" After reading a few lines or a short paragraph, I would despair of trying to understand it, and back it would go, into the "holy of holies" at the head of my bed.

One day the pastor approached our Sunday School class to ask if we would consider baptism. He explained that being baptized meant that you joined the church. We would undergo a six-week course called Catechism. The name sounded a bit scary and the class threatened to be a lot of work, but the need to be religious and do what seemed "right" weighed heavily; after all, it was our Mennonite heritage. Signing up, we learned all about church history, the founders of the Mennonite church and its leaders past and present. At the end of the course, we were baptized with a few drops of water landing on the tops of our heads. Applause followed the announcement that we were now members of the Mennonite church, but I still could not figure out what the connection was to God.

Immediately after the six weeks of catechism, my new faith crashed and the quest for holiness was abandoned. My youngest sister, eleven at that time, was the first one home from school; she found our mother lying in a pool of blood, lifeless. The details have only been imagined, questioning my sister has never been something I could do… or wanted to do. Talking about it only drove spears into our hearts, creating deeper wounds. No one wanted to hurt her, or be hurt further.

That same night, many relatives and church members had gathered at our uncle's house, where my sisters and I were awaiting the arrival of our father. Our own house was covered with detectives and police; blood and

i am scared of the one who holds the key to life

bullet holes were more than we could bear. Unable to sleep, I roamed into the hallway adjacent to the living room where the adults had gathered. I was unseen, but able to hear their conversation when a voice said very clearly, "It must have been God's will!" What? God's will? This was God's will? Alarmed and astonished, it just did not seem possible! And thus, my personal war with God began.

Life became a struggle, like swimming in a warring sea while the lifeguard, God, sat comfortably in the shade relaxing. Our lives were carried out like a robotic routine; our emotions dead, but the finale was yet to come. Two years later, my sister and I and three friends were returning home in a friend's van from a soccer game when a drunken driver trying to pass us rammed into the rear of our car at a high speed, flipping us over and rolling us off the road. All five of us were thrown out of the van. The driver of our car had been my first boyfriend in junior high school… he went through the window of his door and was killed instantly.

23

God was there with us. He was the one who bashed me up against the sides of the car and hurled me out of it unconscious. It was as though he was coaxing me on to hate him even more. Now there was proof that God was after me, not in love, but to kill me, or at least to kill my spirit. He was succeeding. Battered and bruised, expectations for happiness were non-existent. Any hope of a loving God vanished; instead, there appeared a God who was at war.

Beads, long skirts, long hair, and tattered jeans were the fashion of our "freaky," "far-out," hippie generation. We participated in whatever peace movement was happening, marijuana, sit-ins, psychic experimentation, including Ouija boards and séances. The Beatles sang "My sweet Lord… Hari Krishna," and paved the way for our generation to seek truth and enlightenment in yoga and meditation. That era melded me, turning me into who I was… a person trying to find out who I was.

My heart had been set on India for a very long time – desperately wanting to see that dream become reality. It was a search for Truth. With guitar in hand, I left for India, understanding that I was not a priority for God. Still, it did not seem fair that God should get away with quietly disregarding me, or on the other hand, use me for target practice. Trying not to believe in God, but continuing to talk to him, was not a very good way to convince God that he did not exist.

And now these board members were studying me. In the villages, many Indians had never even seen a foreigner, and I was certainly not a very "acceptable" representation of one (hippies being unacceptable to rural India). They feared that my presence could taint the reputation of the children's home! In their hands was the power to decide if I would be allowed to volunteer at Dadiji's children's home for orphans. I was surrounded by people devoted to the God I was running from and it was evident that these people were different from my image of Christians. These people were even more dangerous than I had anticipated, for their faith required one's heart to change… and that was scary. It did not take long to discover that their faith had nothing to do with becoming a "member of the club." Their faith was much more personal, demanding changes that would affect one's whole life.

Scrutinized or not, their hospitality was without fault. The rush to volunteer was somewhat futile; it would take another week for the board to meet and make their final decision regarding my fate. In the meantime, I was obliged to stay with a family who treated me royally (of course). They lived in a wood just below the road, which hugged the side of the mountain as it twisted and turned, winding itself toward the snow-capped Himalayas. The house was on the outskirts of the hill-town called Mussoorie. During that week, they narrated some of their many adventures, quite amazing stories, from people whose lives were completely different from mine. They saw the world so differently… always smiling, always laughing. Had they never faced any loss? Now it became easier to understand a friend who had grown up in India in such a family. He had given me the address of Dadiji's children's

home, saying that it was located in a remote village on the plains. Remote sounded great!

The week in Mussoorie created further opportunity to learn about the home. There was no water, no electricity, no vehicle or telephone, and no one who spoke English. It was important to remain determined and resolute – allowing none of these things scare me. If these Christ-followers could handle the situation, then so could I. However, there was one noticeable difference between them and me. Their reason for living, for doing what they did, was to serve the one they loved more than themselves… Jesus. They were crazy about him. He really was "life" to them. He was their life and without him, they had nothing, but they were happy. Without him, I also had nothing, but I was unhappy. Would I really manage to cope?

Fleeing to the ends of the earth, which was the state of Uttar Pradesh[1] where only .01% of the population in 1974 were Christ-followers, should have made avoiding such people easy, but I seemed to have met all of them. Being a heroine among all these self-sacrificing followers of Jesus was impossible. Forced to devise a defence system; my ploy was to avoid as much conversation as possible, retain a disinterested look, and be ready to 'move out' (physically leave) if the need arose. Why were they always overflowing with love, kindness, and humility? In fact, everyone was ready to go out on a limb for me. They would let their whole day be interrupted to help me out in any way they could. They were not only ready to die for Christ, but if there were ever a need, they would be ready to die for me, too! (That seemed ridiculous, but it was true.) Any cost for them was never too high if it meant serving others. It was the ultimate of attack tactics; no rudeness from me could prevent their love from flowing.

[1] *This area of Uttar Pradesh has more recently become the state of Uttarakhand.*

My destiny was firmly in the hands of people who were obviously reluctant to let me anywhere near an orphan! They even used scare tactics, saying "you will find it too difficult… the area is full of thieves… the children's home staff cannot be trusted… the children are very naughty… you will get lice." I did not even know what lice were! They predicted that my stomach would not be able to take the food. Food seemed of little importance, I was ready to eat anything. There was no vehicle or mode of communication at the home, but none of this affected my determination. At the end of the week, victory was mine and they let me go.

We travelled down the mountain in a Land Rover, through the city of Dehra Dun, across dry riverbeds (about five, which became raging torrents in the monsoon season), and finally on to the compound of the children's home. We seemed to be very far away from civilization. The mountains stood high in the background, but the area surrounding the home was flat, barren and dusty. The whitewashed walls of the buildings were cracked and in need of repair. The home seemed to match the poverty of the surroundings. Still, there was joy to be found in this desert-like village with a hundred orphans surrounding me, far from my enemies. My victory was short-lived. ✌

chapter two

Was it a coma, or a dream-like sort of *déjà vu?* Was this real – was it actually happening to me? Too weak to think straight, I found great relief in letting my mind wander. My ankle-length skirt was crumpled and dusty from sitting on the cement floor all night. The back of my shirt was smudged with creamy powder that had come off the cheaply whitewashed wall I had been leaning against. My hair was uncombed and I was sure Bob could see all the little lice digging through it. I hadn't slept all night and there was an aroma of old sewage on me. It was hard to recall just how I had managed to drag myself into his room early that morning. My body felt strangely heavy, as though it was welded into the bed. I was unable to lift myself. My body seemed to be a gigantic brick which happened to be lying on Bob's bed. Half dazed, I caught him peering at me, asking me something…

"What?" I asked.

His prominent English accent was most annoying. The accent itself wasn't annoying, but Bob was an Englishman down to the core, down to his pastries and tea. He somehow managed to live the life of the elite in our rural, almost primitive setting. Local Indians had already threatened him once, just because he fit so beautifully into the British Raj image. His always polite but often disapproving voice had become very familiar to me. His disapproval of my dishevelled state bore down on me.

"Frieda," he said with finality, "I'm just going to give you a little injection to stop you up".

My mind began to work quickly and I came to my senses with a bit of dread. "Bob," I asked wearily, "have you ever given an injection before?"

There was silence. That was all I needed for an answer. "Great!" I thought to myself, unable physically or mentally to rise to the challenge of stopping him. Closing my eyes, my mind surrendered, "Let it happen... everything else has!"

Stretched out on the wooden rope-strung bed in a tiny rural village of India, I waited for "it" to happen. Once more I allowed myself the privilege of wandering through the past. Here I was, lying helplessly in the middle of all my dreams and aspirations. Helpless? Yes! Unhappy? Not at all! Life was presently in limbo; it was floating millions of miles away from what had been familiar and perching itself in a reality somewhere between dreams and truth. Was this road leading me towards my goal? Was I drawing closer to what "truth" might really be? And was I truly helping the children? Sickness was not a setback along the way, but just one of the many events that was leading me from dream to reality.

"Ouch!" Back in the reality of Bob's little bedroom, he was pulling the needle from my arm. He pressed a wad of cotton on the targeted spot. "That should take effect shortly", he announced. The door burst open and Yip bounced in.

"How are you?" His loud Canadian voice always sounded positive. It always sounded as though it was a happy, smiling sort of voice. It would have been nice to give a happy response, but all I could say was, "Not so great".

"Would you like some tea? How 'bout some toast?"

It was too soon to eat, or even think of food. My body had gone through a night-long cleansing session, and there wasn't an ounce of anything left in me. Propped up on the floor of the bathroom all night, without toilet paper or water, the idea of eating was repulsive. After hearing my cry early that morning, Bob had let me out from behind the locked gate of the girls' dorm. Without waiting for his approval I dragged myself into his bathroom to clean myself up. Now I was a new problem to go along with all the other problems we faced daily at the children's home that Bob, Yip and I were in charge of. A new problem was really just part of the normal daily routine. So, Yip and Bob were investigating the different options they had… would I get better on my own or did I need to go to a hospital? How should they look after me? What medicines should they give me? How could they get me to the hospital? Hmmm… what would they come up with?

There was no electricity, no phone, no car, no motor scooter and no bicycle. We had certainly looked after many sick children; in fact, Yip would carry them on his shoulders to the hospital, which was five kilometres away. In my case, that was not an option! My thoughts were interrupted by Yip's face next to mine as his arms swept underneath my legs and back. He lifted me effortlessly into the air, standing his full six feet two inches. We waltzed through the double screen door of the room. He carried me past a crowd of children staring worriedly and crossed the dusty road to a waiting motor scooter. A young man was seated at the front and Yip placed me directly behind him. One of the older girls, a strong girl, jumped on behind me. "Hang on," was the only caution given to me as the scooter revved its engine and began to move forward.

The scooter had only two seats, but somehow we were all sitting on it. We'd gone about twenty feet when I felt my stomach beginning to heave. I leaned over to vomit, which of course nearly tipped us over. The driver slammed on the brakes and dropped his feet to the ground to balance us. Yip was there in a moment and once again I found myself in his arms. Soon I was back on the same rope bed in Bob's room. I looked up and saw concern on their faces.

"That isn't going to work!" said Yip and was gone.

Left in peace for a short while, I lapsed into a light sleep... until cold little fingers, dirty little fingers, pressed against my forehead. Opening my eyes, Budwara's face was directly above me, staring hard at me; her little fingers continued massaging my forehead. Closing my eyes, I muttered something in Hindi, not even knowing what I'd said. Though I understood very little of the language, we still managed to communicate. In this case, the language of love really worked. Nothing would stop Budwara from serving me, and I wouldn't want to stop her. It was her joy and mine.

Three months passed quickly at the children's home and the children continued to serve me. Everyone wanted to wash my clothes, wash my toes, comb and plait my hair into braids, make my bed and hold my hand. It had become second-hand to hold ten children's hands at one time... one on each finger. I had become accustomed to their grubby hands and runny noses. That was part of who they were. Budwara, whose name means "Wednesday," was always there for me, wanting to be first to serve me. Every night she would be waiting for me to come to bed. Each evening, after the children were asleep, Yip, Bob and I would stay up late talking over the day's happenings and planning for the next day. We would mix powdered milk together with instant coffee, heat it and keep it warm in a teapot, which was a delicacy to be looked forward to. Every night Budwara would be sitting beside my mat on the roof, hers spread out right next to mine, waiting for me, wanting my approval and a little love.

Resting on Bob's bed, her eight-year-old voice mustered all the concerned motherliness it could manage, saying, 'Sisterji, what happened? Why didn't you wake me up last night?' Her little, disapproving voice scolded me, and at the same time, let out a giggle. Her small slanted eyes were bright against her dark face, like stars sparkling against the night sky. Even in her most serious moments, Budwara would let out a little giggle, there was always something that she found somewhere in her spirit to laugh about. Having planned from childhood to look after orphans in India, it was a strangely humorous that now, at the orphanage, I was the one being looked after by a giggle-box orphan. Was that why Budwara had the giggles? Wasn't I supposed to be the angel of mercy, looking lovingly after the children? Deep in Budwara's eyes was a mysterious plan, and a God who laughs in heaven.

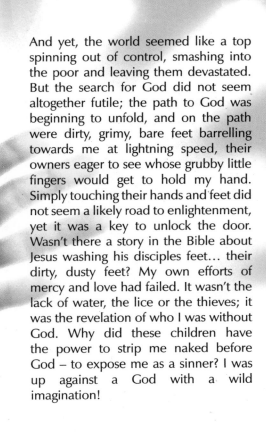

And yet, the world seemed like a top spinning out of control, smashing into the poor and leaving them devastated. But the search for God did not seem altogether futile; the path to God was beginning to unfold, and on the path were dirty, grimy, bare feet barrelling towards me at lightning speed, their owners eager to see whose grubby little fingers would get to hold my hand. Simply touching their hands and feet did not seem a likely road to enlightenment, yet it was a key to unlock the door. Wasn't there a story in the Bible about Jesus washing his disciples feet... their dirty, dusty feet? My own efforts of mercy and love had failed. It wasn't the lack of water, the lice or the thieves; it was the revelation of who I was without God. Why did these children have the power to strip me naked before God – to expose me as a sinner? I was up against a God with a wild imagination!

The double screen doors squeaked as they opened. "Frieda, there is a taxi here to take you to the hospital." Bob was looking official. Yip was standing outside, organizing the children and making sure that the taxi was as comfortable as possible. They helped me to the car.

"The taxi is taking you to Mussoorie," Bob explained, "and the Olsons will meet you there".

As I climbed into the dusty old vehicle, the passenger door opened on the other side. Darshenee, the woman who sat daily to mend clothes, was helping Saroj, the girls' matron, into the back seat beside me. Yip saw the question mark on my face: "She has been unwell for quite a while; we thought it would be a good chance to have her seen by a doctor. Drive straight to the hospital," he added to the taxi-driver. He slapped the car twice to let the driver know he could leave, gave us a smile, and off we went.

Breathing a sigh of relief, we speed off towards our recuperation in the mountains. The Olsons had nursed me and fed me in the past and I was greatly indebted to them already, but I couldn't help looking forward to more of their loving care. Mrs. Olson had even helped clear my head of all its little critters. Such people were hard to find. It was easy to relax now. I reclined in the backseat, and waved goodbye to a hundred dirty little faces.

Why was this happening? Why did this illness seem to be a blessing from God? The poverty and the dirt couldn't have been more real, but what seemed most real was the part I was playing in some sort of invisible school of life with God as the teacher, like my childhood pretend game, only this time it was real. God was definitely not in my pocket. This was one day in a dream that would not be forgotten.

Learning a lot more about Jesus during those three months in the children's home left no doubts; this "faith" that I was hearing about, was something new to my previous understanding. Dadiji, and the other people around me who called themselves disciples of Jesus, or Christ followers, believed that the words of the Bible were the REAL teachings of God, and called Jesus "Saviour". Their church was all around them and their life was caught up in Jesus all the time.

Their devotion to this book, the Bible, was a mystery. The book said that God is love. It said that you must be born again. It said that if we believe Jesus is God and make him Lord of our life, all we have to do is ask him, and he will not only forgive our sins, but also give us eternal life! It sounded like a really good deal, but even so, I was very reluctant to take this step. The simplicity of it all made it sound like a bit of "hocus-pocus". It seemed just as likely to have Cinderella's fairy godmother drop in on me. The Bible makes amazing claims, but where was the proof of all this professed miraculous life-changing power? It was only a book, wasn't it? Perhaps these people were part of a Jesus Christ cult… their belief that Jesus was coming back again was certainly a weird one; he would be coming on the clouds and bringing an army with him! Was the Bible a "holy" science fiction novel, or could it be true?

The reality of my stomach's rumbling brought my thoughts a little closer to earth. What was it that I had eaten? The answer could have been any one of dozens. The kitchen was a building, or more rightly a shack, that was attached to the chicken coop, just next to the buffalo shed. Perhaps it was erected there in order to save the expense of another wall, but the smells coming from the direction of the kitchen were not always pleasant. There were also children who took turns helping the cook by cutting vegetables and rolling the *chapattis* (a flour and water flatbread). It was a position that each of them hoped to get, for it meant the chance of stealing *goor* (sugar) or sneaking a cup of *chi* (tea) or secretly making something extra nice to eat. Working in the kitchen was definitely a position of power. Sometimes the cooks even took a share of the children's food rations for themselves. Without a proper water facility, neither the cooks nor the children could wash their hands before cooking. One could imagine all that went into the well-kneaded *chapatti* dough!

Lack of clean water was the most likely reason for the sickness. To serve one hundred children and staff there was an ox-cart that carried two old oil drums. These were taken to the canal twice daily to bring water for cooking and drinking and toilet use. The canal was about a kilometre away and used by all the villagers and their animals. The boys and girls walked upstream to have their baths; downstream was the area where the buffaloes were bathed, and further downstream was the place where our ox-cart was driven into the water to collect our kitchen's water! That particular spot was chosen because there was no place to drive the oxen into the water upstream. It was bucketed into the oil drums – our drinking water was surely enriched with the best of everything. On the days when the ox-cart could not make the trip to the canal, water was taken from the pond behind the children's home. It was a stagnant green pool with algae along its edges, the water festering with malaria-ridden mosquitoes. The pond smelled as I presently did... like old sewage. (It was also famous for ghosts - white women who floated across its surface at night.)

The resort town of Mussoorie was a place to look forward to. After weeks of eating *chapattis* and *dal* (lentils) very slowly and carefully in order to avoid chipping my teeth on hidden stones, it was a bit of ecstasy to be seated at Mrs. Olson's dining table, eating lemon chiffon pie and tuna sandwiches. Even peanut butter and jelly sounded divine.

Would there be another hair treatment? The last treatment did work... but my "guests" had returned and brought their friends with them. The girls' heads were always full of lice, a problem that I had never before encountered. Being clueless and totally ignorant about how to deal with them, the village technique seemed like the best way to proceed. Like monkeys, we'd all sit in a long line, one in front of the other, patiently searching each other's heads. The offending vermin were pulled out one by one and handed to the person whose hair was being cleaned so she could squish them between her fingernails; this ensured that the "picker"' did not lose her place in her systematic checking. It sounds rather disgusting, but once you became used to it as an accepted method, it was actually a very sociable event. It was a time to relax and talk. Village women worked very hard, and at certain times of the day they would be outside their mud houses sitting on their rope-strung bed, searching through each others hair, enjoying the shade, as well as the gentle massage.

Our taxi passed through the familiar village of Khera. Women relaxed in the

shade, seated on rope beds with their black, oiled hair flowing down their shoulders. The men were squatting on the ground with a *hookah* being passed between them. A *hookah* is a large vase-shaped urn with a long pipe attached from which tobacco, or sometimes hashish, is inhaled. The men, too, looked very relaxed and oblivious to what was happening around them. The mud house behind them was carefully coated with cow dung to make it look clean and well plastered. A deep red henna dye had been used to paint some artistic, geometric designs on the walls and above the door; this helped ward off the evil eye and demonic powers that might enter their home. The children were running around happily, for their parents were preoccupied in their leisure moment, not worried about work. A few barefoot children ran down the road chasing an old bicycle tire, keeping it moving with a stick clutched in their hand. They ran swiftly, but their hair didn't fly; it was stiffly matted and reddish from malnutrition. The bare-bottomed younger children sat in the dirt, wiping their runny noses on their sleeves.

The black Ambassador taxi, the only car in 1974 that was manufactured and sold in India, suddenly swerved to the left as a rickety old bus went speeding by. For a moment all vision was gone and we were enveloped in a cloud of dust. Dust flew in through the window, adding to the already thick layer on the seats. It covered us, but that was no worry. Everything was okay because Mussoorie and a hot shower were now very near. The driver had swerved in order to avoid hitting the mob of people who were hanging out the back door of the bus, which didn't mean that the bus was full. It would soon stop to pick up more passengers; there was still space on the roof amidst the boxes, crates and luggage. That was actually one of the best spots, lots of fresh air and a wonderful view. I had ridden there more than once.

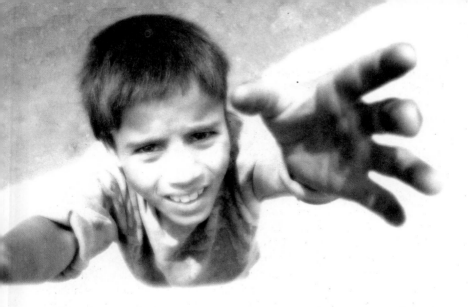

Saroj gazed out of the window and also seemed content to be on her way to Mussoorie. Perhaps Darshenee, who had remained at the children's home, wished she were sick, so that she too, could have had the excuse of going to the mountains. Although the mountains were nearly in her back yard, it was unlikely Darsheenee had ever set foot outside of the village. She was a widow and had two daughters who also lived in the children's home, benefiting from the free food and education. Her husband had been bitten by a cobra and died, leaving her poverty stricken. The village children probably never left their homes except to walk into the village to buy a needed item or collect the mail or bring the water. They did not have the privilege of being taken to a mountain resort town when they were ill. They remained in their homes, lying on the mud floor with flies buzzing around their faces. It had been rumoured that some of them had even died from neglect; it was likely to be true. My mind wandered into the past… was it better to die from a bullet, or from neglect? What kind of grief had I indulged in and claimed to be my right?

Many of the home's staff had no real concern for the welfare of the children; most were there for the job and for whatever they could benefit from. We hadn't actually replaced anyone, but were there to help Dadiji, who had lived on the children's home compound but was forced to leave because of her health. There was no way to know how long it would be before she returned.

We three world travellers had wanted to volunteer. I, an American, had run away from life and from God; Yip, a Canadian, was a high school dropout (whose aim was to be a millionaire); and Bob was a "la-dee-da" Brit who had been demon-possessed. Actually, we were very likely candidates for a God who tends to use the foolishness of "men" for his glory[2]. It was hard for us to believe we were doing what we were doing. We had been in India for just a few months, couldn't speak a (correct) word of Hindi, and no one at the children's home spoke any English. We really didn't know what we were doing, but we were doing something. We were being the best parents that we could be. And isn't that what an orphan needs?

Although, as matron, Saroj was responsible for all of the girls, her own room was far enough away so that she was able live her own life and only get involved with the girls when she decided to do so. I stayed with the girls, for no other room had been offered to me. It was one very large room, housing all fifty of us. Originally, it had been two rooms, but a large hole had been made in the dividing wall, like a broken picture window; it looked as though a bomb had exploded there and no one had bothered to fix it. Outside was a long veranda that overlooked the compound. Another flight of stairs led to the roof, where the girls sometimes played and where we slept on hot summer nights. Each person had a bamboo mat or a thin cotton mattress to spread on the rough cement (providing a small amount of comfort) and a sheet to cover with. A waist-high wall

[2]   *He chose what the world looks down on and despises, and thinks is nothing, in order to destroy what the world thinks is important. This means that no one can boast in God's presence. I Cor. 1:28 – 29*

was all that separated us from a drop of three floors. Some of the girls had the reputation of dropping puppies off the roof. Why? It was hard to imagine why they did that. Perhaps they were trying to get revenge for their own hurts. It certainly dashed my childhood ideas of innocent little orphans.

The boys, fifty of them, were located on the other side of the compound. They had a few more rooms than the girls, but the accommodation was no better; in fact, in some ways it was worse. Because the boys occupied many rooms it was dangerous; it meant an easy route for abuse from staff or even older boys. Similar to the girls' matron, the dorm parents lived in a separate house and didn't take time to find out what happened in the boys' rooms.

Moving into a room with fifty girls who spoke a language I could not understand, left me a little unsure of what kind of approach to use. My possessions were very few, but as a foreigner, whatever I owned tended to stand out just because it was different. So, I decided to display everything. There was a long, open shelf above my bed, perfect for my display. Everything – ornament to underwear, was neatly laid out there, including my watch. We had an unspoken agreement; the girls never touched anything without permission, but they were allowed to take turns wearing my watch.

Making shelf space that was "mine" led me to realize that none of the girls had their own space for anything, which was partly why they never knew which clothes were theirs. There was an unused closet with lots of shelf space. I cleaned it out and bought some black paint. Each one was given a space to keep their clothes with their names boldly written underneath to mark their new, private spots. The girls loved to read their names written on the wall. It may have been the first time they actually felt a bit of ownership towards the building that was their "home". It certainly helped to keep them organized and clean.

As the car manoeuvred its way through Dehra Dun, heat emanated from the buildings and penetrated our tired bodies. My sweaty body was soaking up dirt like a mop. Dehra Dun was not a large city geographically, but it had a population of about a quarter of a million people. One could easily walk the length and breadth of it in a day. It was known as a beautiful city because of its climate and its backdrop – the magnificent Himalayan mountain range, whose peaks are snow covered year round. In the summer Dehra Dun remained cooler than most areas of India and was very cold in the winter. It was, and is still today, known for having some of the best schools in all of India.

Mussoorie, a hill station, sits at 7,000 feet above sea level and is located in what are called the foothills of the Himalayas (7,000 feet being only a bump against what lies behind it). The road to this hill-station is extremely curvy; as good as any roller coaster, and its curves were beginning to make an impact on my stomach. (The Olsons nicknamed the road *"jalebee road"*. *Jalebees* are Indian sweets, deep-fried and soaked in sugar syrup, shaped like circles in circles, going round and round.) Landslides are a regular occurrence in the monsoon and travel can be blocked for hours. The air blowing into the car windows became cooler and the taxi began to swerve from one side to the other. It was just as well that my stomach was already empty. Every other car or bus we met had someone sticking their head out the window throwing up. We passed a few large grey monkeys sitting along the side of the road. Later, we passed through the market area where smaller, reddish-brown monkeys hung from wires and ran along roofs, begging from storekeepers for a treat. Nearly all the way

up, the road's edge was a straight drop down, often plummeting hundreds of feet. More than a few buses had gone over the edge. Still, there was no reason to worry. This was India, and from where I had been previously to where I was going now, that seemed crazy in itself. It seemed as if I was not only the star of a movie, but was also the audience, sitting back and watching the story unfold. Yes, I could just take whatever came my way. There were lots of things to think about. People had opened my eyes, daring me to reconsider my own ideas and life values, people who had challenged the lack of truth in my life, people like Chotu.

Chotu was a little boy who lived in the children's home. Because he was the youngest, he lived on the girls' side so that he would receive a bit more mothering. Chotu was four years old and an albino. His white skin and shiny white clump of tangled hair, his bright red eyes and his continually sad face made an impact on anyone who saw him. Not many people saw him, for he was neatly tucked into the darker corners of the orphanage.

From a young age, I had practiced loving orphans through my 'pretend' game, and thought it would be easy, but loving Chotu tore me apart. Loving Chotu was like looking in a mirror. I looked him in the eyes, but saw only my own frustrations, my own poverty, my own shortcomings, and I didn't know what to do with him or with myself. His life called for a response that I could not come up with.

He wasn't the same as the other children on the outside, and was somehow different on the inside as well. He looked at you very deeply through his red eyes and his huge round sunglasses, which made him look a bit like a chipmunk. We had bought him the large, round plastic glasses, hoping that they would render the sun less hard on his eyes. He always squinted as though it hurt. It really did hurt - the world, that is.

He was always crying. His nose always seemed to be running, and he always had diarrhoea. He was not a pleasant sight and I didn't like what I saw. Because he was somewhat repulsive to me, he made me repulsive to myself. Clearly, I was a reflection of the world; no different from others who hadn't come to India to look after orphans, for I was like the rest of the world. I wasn't the world's answer for loving the orphans. The scary part was that I could see myself for who I was, and there was a lot of lack.

you held children on your lap

It brought into focus much of what the Olsons had been talking about. They argued that they would be willing to die for Jesus. Die for Jesus! They were willing to die for someone who is invisible, someone who is, at best, a sort of ghost or spirit. To be honest, when I looked at this child I found myself not even wanting to touch him. His deep needs tore at my heart, but left me wanting. I was not ready to die for anyone, not for this child, and certainly not for a ghost. That thought did not seem right, or righteous, and it brought me face to face with sin, a Bible word that was not "relevant" to the hippie world. Surely I was not *bad*… I had good ideals and good values, and I was living out my values. So why did I always come up lacking? Why did I feel so awful, so unclean? Why did it seem that somehow I had missed the point? There surely had to be more to life than what I was putting into it. I hoped so for the sake of the children, and for the sake of Chotu.

The engine revved hard as the car strained sharply upward on a steep hill. Twice we stalled, backed up, and did a three-point turn in a minuscule area. Once more we climbed sharply upward. In another minute the car came to a halt.

The driver jumped out and helped us out of the car. We'd reached the hospital. It stood three storeys high, backed up upon the edge of the mountain. We were ushered in and given multiple blood tests.

Unfortunately, they admitted me into the ward instead of sending me off to the Olsons house... no hot showers or lemon pies. Instead, a needle was stuck in my arm, which slowly dripped glucose sugar into my body... I'd lost fifteen pounds overnight.

In a moment, Dr. Olson walked in: "Well, Frieda, so nice to see you again!" And he gave a chuckle through his big grin. I smiled back, able to see in the warmth of Dr. Olson a clearer image of the person I really was, which wasn't that great, but I sensed that God saw me in the same way – not perfect, but loved by him just as I was. I realized that from the time I had arrived at the children's home, God had loved me with great mercy, no matter how lacking I was in mercy, or how bad I was or how bad I looked (and I'm talking about my heart, for I know that is what God looks at), and no matter what lack of love there was in me, God loved me... the person who was running from him and hating him. And again, here I was, resting in his arms. The hospital bed wasn't exactly what I think of as the arms of God, but the security I felt in the midst of chaos had to be God.

A long weekend was spent in the hospital gaining back my strength. Saroj was diagnosed with tuberculosis and was treated and sent to her hometown for another six months of rest and medicines. She never returned to the children's home. Arriving back to the home a week later, I became the new matron. I watched myself stepping heroically into a new movie, and wondered what in the world I was going to do. I hoped that God would be there. ❀

chapter three

Within the first few days after arriving in India, Yip had entered my new world. At that time he was living in Mussoorie, helping Dr. Olson with his clinics. We met in the house where he and a couple other workers lived. He was sitting on a tall stool and leaning into the corner, his long legs stretched out in front of him. The cigarette perched upon his lips didn't interfere with his smile. His eyes seemed to go very deep, sculpted like two caves underneath his forehead; he always said it was the "Neanderthal Look". In any case, he seemed to be looking out of them from somewhere deep within. He wore jeans, or more accurately, patches, as there was no place left on his jeans that were "jean". Frizzy hair dangled in tangles at his shoulders - for me it could have been love at first sight, but to my great surprise and disappointment, he too, was a follower of Jesus. Any romantic thoughts were immediately dismissed and he had to be counted as "one of them"… albeit a unique one.

Yip left Canada in 1971, but he had left his Toronto home much earlier. His real name was Ken, and that was what his large family called him. They were six brothers and one sister. His mother made sure that each one of them learned how to provide for themselves by ensuring they learned how to contribute to the family at a young age. By the time Ken turned sixteen, he was well trained for survival, and ready to try life on his own.

The moment he turned the correct legal age to leave home, he hitchhiked west, crossing Canada and then south to California. Drugs and drinking played a major role in his trip, but one day Ken miraculously came to his senses and remembered that school had started. He phoned his parents and told them that he was coming home. He arrived back two months late for school. Instead of moving back into his home, Ken decided to live at the hippie commune where his older brother was. He faithfully did his part in contributing towards the needs of communal life; in fact, work became the priority and he attended school only when he had time.

He secured a very good job in a well-known restaurant chain. He was a favourite of the restaurant owner, the third richest man in Toronto and a millionaire. Ken worked very hard, rightfully earning the boss's admiration, often staying at the job through the night and into the early hours of the morning. He was soon managing one of the restaurants on his own. Quite often, the boss would invite him to his penthouse apartment to drink with him. After many drinks his boss would loosen up and begin complaining about his many ex-wives who had married him for his money. He bemoaned the fact that everyone was after his money. Ken sympathized with him the best he could, knowing full well that he too, was after his money. Although one of Ken's aims was to become the world's youngest millionaire, he found the times with his boss very disturbing. Judging from the life of his boss, money seemed to have nothing to do with happiness; it appeared that the opposite was true.

When Ken started talking about taking time off to travel, his boss set up another restaurant job for him in the Fiji Islands. Ken had been in the restaurant business for almost six years, and this seemed like a good time to leave if he were to see the world. The working world would just have to wait for him.

REND YOUR HEART

He travelled to England, then overland to Europe and across to the Middle East. In those days there was a well-used hippie trail, which guaranteed many great adventures, and Ken experienced two major ones before reaching India. The first one took place in Switzerland at a community called L'Abri, founded by the late author and lecturer, Francis Schaeffer. The community thrived on apologetics and the intellectual understanding of Christ and the Bible.

After attending some of the lectures Ken couldn't find any fault with their philosophies, for there was certainly substantial reason to believe the Bible as authentic history - other historical sources backed it up. Furthermore, the Old Testament found its prophecies fulfilled with the coming of Jesus… each and every one of them. This meant there was good reason to believe that Jesus was the Son of God. Ken adopted this new thinking and was soon calling himself a Christian. It created no problems until he reached Israel.

The community of international volunteers on the kibbutz suited Ken, but his name did not suit them. He developed a deep friendship with a kibbutz family, who claimed "Ken" was a very silly name, for in Hebrew it means "yes!" So, he was given a "proper" name, at least in their thinking – "Yip", because it was the word Ken always used instead of "yes". His kibbutz mother approved of the name, for she was Dutch and "Yip" had a definite Dutch ring to it. The name stuck.

At the kibbutz, Yip made an effort to continue with his new faith and yet remain part of the hippie culture. At first it created no problems… after all, California was alive with a new generation of God-fearing hippies called "Jesus Freaks." Yip's outlook on life had changed, but his habits had not. Faith, he reasoned, meant following Christ, which he understood as a change in thinking. Unfortunately, a purely intellectual understanding of faith didn't hold out for him in real life.

A few weeks after his arrival an alarm sounded all over Israel. All foreigners were issued a warning to leave immediately and given a short period of time to do so, for the country was fast becoming bogged down in a war. The Yom Kippur war had begun and every Israeli, male and female, between the ages of eighteen and fifty was called to fight. Yip had developed a very close relationship with the sons of his kibbutz family; one of them was in the military when the war broke out. The oldest son was living in Australia, but when the war began; he immediately returned to Israel to fight, as did many other Israelis, flying in from all over the world. The only people left on the kibbutz were the very young and the very old.

Yip's heart went out to these people who had opened their homes to him. He decided to remain on the kibbutz, working hard to cover the neglected daily chores that needed attention. The Yom Kippur war was Israel's biggest tank war, and there were many casualties. News arrived all too quickly; Yip's friend, the second son, had been killed in a tank. The family was devastated. In their youth, the parents of the family, Asher and Tamar, had been prisoners in a Nazi concentration camp in Germany, miraculously escaping with their lives while most of their extended families died. They had fought to make Israel a nation, and poured out their hearts while smuggling many Jews to safety, risking their lives constantly. Their spirits had died many times over. For them, the hardest part was holding on to the desire to go on living. And now, the news of their son came like a knife stabbing them in the back.

Yip also had to find a way to fight his grief and anger. He stayed for another six months on the kibbutz to help in whatever way he could. Then he picked up his Bible, scratched out his name in the front of it, dumped it into the kibbutz library and headed for India.

Arriving on the banks of India's sacred river, the Ganges, Yip was approached by *sadhus* and *gurus*[3] who wished to lure him into their ashrams for yoga and meditation. Hippie travellers were constantly looking for a way to get out of their world and into another. Drugs were one route, but some chose the eastern way of reaching enlightenment. It wasn't long before Yip began to look for another environment. He'd heard of the Olsons, who had set up medical clinics in the Himalayas, and he went in search of them, hoping they needed a volunteer; free room and board were always a drawing card. In dirty, patched clothes, smelling of the previous months of travel, he arrived on their doorstep... the same doorstep that I first arrived on! To his surprise he was greeted like a long lost friend. They assured him that they would really appreciate his help, and so began his "medical" career, working in their clinics.

[3] *Hindu holy men*

Every view from the house in Mussoorie where Yip roomed with three others was spectacular. The front side of the house looked over a valley and across to the plains, where distant lights sparkled, exhibiting the cities below. The other side of his house boasted a fantastic display of proud snow-capped peaks. One starry night in Mussoorie, Yip looked down over the deep valley and then gazed upwards at the night-lights. Out of nowhere he heard a voice saying, "Will a person gain anything if he wins the whole world but loses his life? Of course not! There is nothing he can give to regain his life." He swung himself around to see who was

In Me I Find The Need For You

there. No one was present. He was amazed. He had heard the voice so clearly. He went into his room and searched his Bible. Sure enough, he found the verse in Matthew 16:26. He tried to sleep but could not even close his eyes; it was as though someone was continuously pestering him that night. Early in the morning it dawned on him who it was… God! Yip prayed, "God, I can't even imagine why you're after someone like me, but if you really want me, I'm yours". That was all he needed to say. Nothing would ever be the same again.

When Yip and I met, he had just walked into a new life, and I had no idea that a great spiritual transformation was happening in that longhaired hippie. He, too, had been touched by God's undivided love; we were beginning to have an understanding of God's love working itself out in our lives... showing itself in the most unexpected places. God was after us. He was continually following us. God was following us? Wasn't it supposed to be the other way around?

bound to love mysteriously

Bob was one of Yip's housemates, a very different character from Yip. When I first met Bob, he too, was a very new follower of Jesus. He was definitely a changed man if what I heard about him was true… and no one seemed to lie. Bob also confessed to me that what I'd heard was the truth; his father was a warlock and his mother was a witch! He could not remember a time in his life when he did not have a spirit accompanying him. Earlier it had been evil spirits, but now it was the Holy Spirit. While staying in Mussoorie, evil spirits inside of him made their presence known, and after being counselled, he agreed to be exorcised. Some of the believers in God gathered together and prayed over him in the name of Jesus; for hours his demons put up a good fight, but were finally cast out. During the exorcism Bob actually slithered around on the floor like a snake and marched up and down the room yelling out orders in German (a language he doesn't know) as though he were Hitler, and finally collapsed on the floor, having only the energy of Bob left in him. After many long years, Bob was free to be Bob, only Bob, and we all discovered what a nice and pleasant person

The third person staying with Yip had a very short name: P.M. He was from south India, a person with an amazing amount of love and a great servant heart. He was the house "leader" and had his work cut out for him. P.M. was the one who had to keep peace and unity, for Yip and Bob were poles apart in personality and had regular clashes with each other. P.M. remained calm; he could so easily bring in a sound word of advice, and with a very light heart make everyone laugh and relax. He patiently helped them and taught them what they were up against spiritually. When Bob's demonic manifestations came out, his ability to explain the powers and authorities of darkness not only brought in understanding, but also brought forgiveness and love with the truth that all are sinners and all are fighting the same enemy of God, Satan. In God, a place for unity and love was found.

P.M. also made it a point to come to the orphanage and spend time helping me with whatever questions I wanted an answer for. Often, when P.M. or the Olsons would come down to the children's home, they would invite

me to come back to Mussoorie with them. It was always a longed-for, needed break for me. It was during one of those times, a few weeks after my illness, and during one of those greatly looked forward to meals, that a miracle took place.

Yip and Bob had joined me at the orphanage two months after my initial arrival, making it possible for me to visit the Olsons occasionally. It was on one of those nights, during their after-dinner family devotions that Psalm 139 was read. Heaving a reluctant sigh, I sat back, trying my best to become part of the chair, hoping to be 'excluded' from too much of the interaction, but as they read, I sat spellbound. It was amazing that the Psalm they read was describing me! It said that there was no place to hide from God because he was always present everywhere. I could not escape even if I ran to the ends of the earth for he would still find me there! (I really knew about that!) I hadn't read much of the Bible, but it seemed to be describing me. I tried to hide my interest, but couldn't wait to get away to my room that night to read more from the Bible.

Sacrificial Love ...

Alone in my room, I read until early morning... until I could hold my eyes open no longer. Having had no idea where to begin, I'd started at the beginning: "In the beginning, when God created the universe..." (Gen.1:1) and on it went – God created a man, and then a woman, and finally I read that; "The man and the woman were both naked, but they were not embarrassed." (Gen. 2:25)

Reading Genesis, I suddenly felt naked; guilt, fear and pride had been exposed and I was ashamed. My façade was quickly being erased, leaving me with nothing, except me. The huge wall that I had built around me began to crumble before my very eyes. I wanted to cry out, "BUT I DON'T WANT JESUS!" But what if God was actually listening? All my good intentions, my good will, my righteous desires... all seemed now to be marked with arrogance and pride. The truth of my heart had first been unveiled through the children, and again laid bare through this weird and wonderful book, God's Word, which had come alive for me that night

a choice not just for me.

as a living history, a history that was somehow waiting to write me into it! But the most compelling thought, the most persuasive fear, was that it was God who was after me! I was beginning to see myself for who I was. I realized that my display of non-interest in Christ wasn't the truth. I was interested. I really wanted to know if what the Bible said was true.

The mystery of this ghost story, the Holy Ghost story, was reaching a climax, and just might be solved. Some people describe the Holy Spirit as "our conscience", but why then, do people crave for God, and why do we yearn for eternity? Where does our strong sense of right and wrong come from? Why do we attach right and wrong with eternal judgment? Is there a judge? If our values come from our conscience, then who knew the values to put into our conscience? In the Bible it is written that Jesus breathed on his disciples, telling them to receive the Holy Spirit, and with that heavenly kiss, voilà! They had the Spirit of God inside of them... a spirit they did not have before.

for you NOW is the time

As a child, I had prayed fervently for my doll to be made alive, but I hadn't realized that for God, I was his "doll". I was the child, the one he loved and on whom he wanted to breathe his life-giving Spirit. He wanted me to become alive, alive through a second birth – a spiritual birth. I hadn't understood that the prayer for my doll could come true for myself. God was truly after me with undivided love, to breathe into me that life-giving kiss, the gift of himself, his Spirit, the Holy Ghost.

The Olsons had a home-library, which they were very proud of. High shelves of books on faith met whoever entered their home. Being a reader, I couldn't resist searching their shelves for something that would occupy some of my free moments. Before I left their house that weekend, I searched those shelves for an interesting book to take with me. Normally, I would skim over any obviously Christian title, but there was little else to look at. That day a book caught my eye; it was entitled *Sadhu Sundar Singh*. It was about an Indian *sadhu*, and this book looked like it could be interesting.

He was a *sadhu*, a guru, who wore the honoured and highly respected saffron robes. He walked barefoot across India and into Tibet and lived a life close to God. He was born as a Sikh. His family being part of a very religious community, the Sikh teachings had been driven into him from a young age; however, as a child he attended a Christian school. There he developed an interest in the Bible's teachings, but at the same time became disillusioned. What was Truth? Whom to believe? His search for God became desperate, which led to a desperate decision; one morning he lay down on a railway track to wait for the morning train… if God did not show himself, he would end his life there. Lying on the tracks at dawn, Sundar Singh had a vision of Jesus on the cross and immediately dedicated his life to God, as one of his followers. His family was livid and poisoned him, forcing him to flee in a dangerously weak state. He eventually collapsed but was found by Christians who nursed him back to health.

Like a child, I see your face

At that point in the book, I had to set it down in order to do some serious thinking. Wasn't I also searching for God? Hadn't I also told him to reveal himself to me numerous times? Why should God meet someone else and avoid me? What does it take to get God's attention? Sundar Singh's life amazed me. He walked barefoot through dark jungles and across the high snow-covered Himalayas, talking to God as he went, like talking to a familiar friend. He actually knew God. Everything in the Bible led me to believe that it was possible for me, or anyone to have a relationship with God, just as close a relationship as Sadhu Sundar Singh had, and even closer than the relationship I had with my own father. Did God want to be as close to me as he was to Sundar Singh? Would God be my friend? Could I really be his child and he, my father? The real question was up to me to answer: Could I let go of my pride and actually give myself wholly to Jesus?

God knew me very well; in fact, God was intimately acquainted with me, just like Psalm 139 says. And why shouldn't my creator know me? That long awaited moment became so simple! Closing the last page of the book, I felt that deep yearning springing up in my heart, a yearning that had been there for a long time. "God," I cried, "that is what I want! This is the relationship I want with you; I want to be your close friend!" In a few seconds God answered and I felt the Holy Spirit stirring inside of me. The joy in my spirit was out of control and I jumped up and sprang around the room. Something was happening in me that wasn't me! This was the beginning of an end. It ended my search to identify God, but it was the beginning of a new life with God – not the end of seeking a relationship. God and I were just beginning a friendship, and I knew there was a lot more life to come.

After my return to the children's home, God began laying a foundation in my life, just as he had been doing for Bob and Yip. We three were an unlikely team to end up running a children's home, but God was rooting us in him for the future, and using us as his vessels in the present, weak clay vessels, filled with Holy Spirit power! Yip's travels had led him down a path where his desires were now far from what he had originally been aiming for; it was a complete turn-around from wanting to be a millionaire! On the other hand, he never would have owned the riches of sacrificial love if he had lived only as he wished, but he had set foot in an orphanage and felt compassion for the poor. Had Bob never met the Holy Spirit, demons would still be controlling his life. And for my part, if my dream had remained only to serve the orphans of India, I would not only have been a slave to good works and missed out on what life is about, but I would also have denied the value of Christ's death on the cross, and in doing so denied myself a relationship with God.

Suffering and sacrificial love were not concepts we were familiar with before meeting God, but they were concepts laid down in Jesus before the foundations of the earth. We had so much to learn! As new disciples of God, we were constantly discovering the depths of his love, drawn from a well with limitless water. God's greatest sacrifice, the sacrifice of Jesus himself, was linked to our own spirits – love embraced through suffering. It had made no sense to us until, by faith, we saw Jesus dying on the cross. Why had we assumed life would always be easy? Jesus suffered deeply and called us his followers. We had committed ourselves to be his disciples, a vow not unlike a marriage vow, in sickness and in health, for better or worse. Where would the road take us? What was this rather extreme training preparing us for in the future? It was hard to guess, but one thing was certain, we could not go back to living life without God.

So, what happened at the children's home? If I told you what happened you may not believe me (just like those English women); but what happened was this: Yip, Bob and I grew in our relationship with God; we faced many trials, from difficult living, to sickness, beatings and jail. We saw miracles, trod on scorpions (literally) and saw angels… yes, it sounds dramatic, but miracles are only the normal promises of God to those who trust in him. I'll finish with just one more story.

Certainly God was the one who transformed our lives, but Bob should be given at least a little bit of credit. It was Bob who "got the ball rolling." Because of Bob, the future was changed. Bob had always wanted to get married, and was regularly falling in love. Marriage was on his mind. Yip and I were constantly involved with the children and the many little problems that were part of their lives. For us, every day felt like it was being played in fast forward, leaving us no time to relax. Bob, however, was able to see what we never saw. In fact, he took on the role of a good Indian father (with a British accent), and cleverly planned some matchmaking.

My visa was nearly finished, so two weeks before I had to leave India, he came to me. "Frieda," he said with a tone of voice that declared authority, "I think you should start praying..."
("Now what is he going to say?" I mused.)
"... Because Yip is going to ask you to marry him!"
Wow! Now that was not what I thought he would say! Should I believe him or not? How had he arrived at this rather personal information?

After this little conversation, he secretly went trotting off in Yip's direction. "Yip," he said sternly, "open up your eyes! Don't you see her across the compound?" That must have shocked Yip, because he started looking across the compound, and within another week, two days before I had to leave India, Yip and I met for chi at a tiny shop in the village and walked out of it engaged.

Two lines formed... two very long rows of dusty feet and dirty hands, each set of ten fingers eagerly holding their dented tin plates. Each face carried a look of anxious excitement, and every eye was peering over the next person's shoulder to get a glimpse of the new couple who sat proudly at the end of the lines. He wore striped *pajamas*, yes, he really did, and a white *khadi kurta,* the pride of India. It was the typical village dress, which all the men in the village wore. I wore a plain green cotton *salwar kurta,* the dress of the local village women. My black hair was in two braids, tied together at the back of my neck with a bright red ribbon from the girls, the ribbon every schoolgirl in India wore daily woven into her braids. Draped around my neck and lacing my head were necklaces of tiny wild flowers, which the girls had picked from the sides of the road. It was the end of June, the hottest time of the year, and noontime, the hottest time of the day. We had cast our rubber slippers to the side and sat barefoot and cross-legged together on the warm cement outside the school as huge cooking vessels, black from the soot of the wood fires, were placed before us. The engagement party had begun! That was a very special party, for it was also a celebration of new life within us, and the anticipation of new life to come. ❧

a few words afterwards

We come to the end, as well as the beginning of the story; there is so much more I could write. Over the years Yip and I have done our share of questioning God when our prayers seemed unheard. We've seen six of the children we raised in our children's home die, but we have also seen miracles. We've seen God heal diseases for which there was no cure and have seen people set free from demonic spirits. We've grown in faith as we've seen the power of God revealed in answered prayer. For us, the most amazing thing is that Yip and I – two normal people loaded down with all the big and little problems life dishes out – personally met the God of creation. It happened because we decided to acknowledge God… a small thing to do for an almighty God! It all started when we were young (newborns in Christ) and had no idea what we were doing (no exaggeration). How? God! Knowing God is gaining knowledge that previously we never knew existed, learning of the invisible reality which is more real than anything we can see with our eyes; for this present earth will pass away, and eternity will take its place[4]. Knowing God gives us a healthy respect of death, for we recognize what "life" really is.

[4] *Then I saw a new heaven and a new earth. The first heaven and the first earth disappeared, and the sea vanished. And I saw the Holy City, the new Jerusalem, coming down out of heaven from God, prepared and ready, like a bride dressed to meet her husband. I heard a loud voice speaking from the throne: "Now God's home is with mankind! He will live with them, and they shall be his people. God himself will be with them, and he will be their God. He will wipe away all tears from their eyes. There will be no more crying or pain. The old things have disappeared." (Rev. 21:1-4)*

According to the Bible, death means living eternity separated from God in Hell, Satan's domain, where there will be no rest, only pain. Did you know that you don't have to die? Death is a choice, for if we know Christ, our physical death is turned into life. Heaven or hell is a choice that God left with us, for God composed this world's ending at the same time that he began creating it[5], purposing everything in it for a salvation much larger than our imagination can comprehend.

"*I consider that what we suffer at this present time cannot be compared at all with the glory that is going to be revealed to us...*

For we know that up to the present time all of creation groans with pain, like the pain of childbirth. But it is not just creation alone which groans; we who have the Spirit as the first of God's gifts also groan within ourselves, as we wait for God to make us his sons and set our whole being free."

(Romans 8 vs. 18, 22 - 23)

[5] *The wisdom I proclaim is God's secret wisdom, which is hidden from mankind, but which he had already chosen for our glory even before the world was made. (I Cor. 2:7)*

Years ago, when my children were young, Nibha, the youngest, had a question. She asked me, "If God did not make the earth, then what would be here?" (Only a child could ask such a question!) Not having the answer, I replied that it was a hard question and I did not know. That was not good enough for her five-year-old curiosity. "No, Mommy! What would be here… a big hole or something?" Again, I told her I really couldn't say. "Then", she said resolutely, "when I get to heaven I'm gonna' ask God what would be here".

One of her older sisters laughed and teased, "Yeah, sure! Do you think God is gonna' tell you?" At that, Nibha looked surprised and turned to me, "If I ask God, he will tell me, won't he?"

As soon as she had asked, I knew that God would tell her. I felt a bit jealous of her child-like faith in God, whom she trusted as her father. She knew her Father very well, and knew that she could ask him anything. Jesus did not enter into the world as a superhero. He was the servant of all, the son of a labourer. He dined with sinners and died with criminals. Jesus came to us in human form, in flesh, sweat, and tears, so that we could meet him and not be afraid, allowing us to step boldly into an intimate relationship with God, which Jesus' life, death and his resurrection have opened up for us. He showed us again and again, to assure us beyond any doubt, that he really does love us just as we are. He leaves no way to attain heights

FATHER

LORD, KEEP ME AS YOUR CHILD, FOR MY HEART CALLS OUT

of spirituality; instead, he invites us to come to him like a child, just as we are, for he not only longs to embrace us, but also wants our love in return.

Who wouldn't want the joy of feeling safe in arms that can carry us through any storm? God, who desires us, plants and nurtures these desires in our hearts and spirits. Is God seducing us? The thought of "seduction" may not be taught in Bible seminaries, but it is certainly what the Bible says: the word of God confirms it over and over again – God loves us and wants us to love him. His 'mission' from the very beginning, is to woo us into loving him. God is after us. Whether you are young and find it hard to live up to the image of today's heroes, or whether you are old and watching the wrinkles beginning to take over your face, God's love is continually that of a father to his child. He died for us, a desperate act and a planned attack, to woo us into loving him and open the way to heaven… to him. His love is timeless and changeless, totally unconditional. He is a jealous God and is passionately after all our attention.

Anyone who takes a step of faith, small or large, is able to embrace God's promises and see them become reality in their own life. Miracles are guaranteed, for with the new believers first step of faith, God sends his

Holy Spirit and he is "born again" – the first miracle! God's promise is to continue working in us, drawing us into a more intimate relationship with himself. It is a promise that we can hold him to; a promise not depending on anything we do – whether it is deserved or not; for the only thing we sinners deserve is death. But God's extravagant forgiveness defeated death on the cross and made eternal life in heaven ours, if we want it.

Faith lives inside those who trust in God as a daily, practical, spiritual discipline. Every day can become a step closer in a relationship with God. The promise of God is that the lame will walk and the blind will see, demons will be cast out and we will see Jesus. Our view is obstructed and our faith is weak because of what we can see – a chaotic, seemingly meaningless world; but his promise to us is that one day we will see him as he is, face to face in all his glory; and then, the reality of eternity will be clear.

One morning I awoke with a thought running through my head, like the making of a song: *I release your spirit to soar the skies.* My oldest daughter Kirti was graduating from high school. In my heart I knew that was exactly what I had to do for her. Suddenly Kirti bounced into the bedroom and clapped her hands together dramatically: "Mom, I can't believe it! My life is just beginning. I can do so much now! Just think… wouldn't it be wonderful if I could die for Jesus?"

"Whoa! Slow down! Let your life begin before you die for Jesus!"

Kirti[6] was feeling ready to tackle the world, a feeling I could understand. Her perspective, though, was very different from what mine had been at her age. Her highest goal was to die for Jesus. Although the thought of her early death went against everything in me, I knew that I had to release her to her dreams, for they were good aspirations. There she was, jumping up and down clapping her hands with joy at the thought of dying for Jesus! She would graduate from high school in two days, and even in all her innocence and naivety; I had to release her to capture her dreams, just as God had released me to capture mine.

[6] Kirti and her husband are now living in a remote area of China.

Now a thought runs through my head; it's the making of a song, not just for Kirti or Yip, but also for everyone and for me. It has a very urgent beginning, like a heart-felt plea longing to be heard and recognized as truth:

> *I release your spirit to soar the skies,*
> *I release your desires to meet your God on high,*
> *I release your dreams to be fulfilled,*
> *I release you.*

Yip is soaring, my children – Sonu, Kirti, Asher, Sheva and Nibha, are soaring, and I, too, have taken flight. The edge of the cliff is there, but we have learned the secret; it is not this world that is life threatening, but the danger of losing our souls and never knowing the love of God. So I release my family to their dreams, and I also release myself. With God's release, we are freed to live and die for sacrificial love.

touch the feet
for you are made from dust
you know that the one who walked in dirt
has his throne on
holy ground
so
touch the feet

"But by the free gift of God's grace all are put right with him through Christ Jesus, who sets them free."

Romans 3:24

the End

about the author

by Phil Leighton

I first met Ken and Frieda McRae in 1990 when a friend took me to visit the children's home they had begun in 1978 in the foothills of the Himalayas. My initial experience wasn't good; instant culture shock, on entering India, and major stomach upset had me hating India and longing for home after only four days. Three weeks later, when I arrived back in England, I knew I had to go back to revisit the McRaes and the children's home – a longing that is still with me sixteen years, and fourteen visits later.

What brought about my change of heart after my initial trip to India? It was largely due to a growing love for the McRaes, their family, and for the boys in the home who had become a part of me – a relationship that has

Ken and Frieda McRae

continued to grow over the years. The atmosphere was so wonderful; I was touched by the fact that Ken and Frieda's children, Sonu, Kirti, Asher, Sheva and Nibha, and the boys in the home were all treated as family, living together in one large house, playing together and also working on the farm together. I remember sitting with Ken, watching the boys play cricket and asking him, "which team are you supporting?" His reply was "they're all my boys, how can I support one side and not the other?" Later, when their family was living on the first floor of a smaller house and above a group of the older teenage boys, Ken would go downstairs every evening to spend time with those boys and, at least once a week, they'd be invited upstairs for a meal; what fun they had as they all sat around the table together.

I was amazed that this couple who had come to India, separately, on the hippy trail and had found Jesus and each other while helping care for needy kids had chosen to obey God by dedicating their lives to working with these, sometimes unlovely, children. Amazed, too, at their incredible vision and capacity (through God) to turn the dream into reality. Presently, the home has around 50 boys, ranging in age from four to twenty, all from different backgrounds, but each needing the same love and stability that the community offers. The campus has fields for crops and vegetables, a fruit orchard, a dairy with a dozen or more cows, a growing school for children from the home and from the surrounding village area, and various buildings, which serve the children and staff of the community. Where did Ken (the high school drop-out) learn the building, farming, pastoral and counselling skills that permitted the growth and success of the home? His answer has always been that whenever he needed knowledge, God would send someone to him, and as he and Frieda and their co-workers prayed, God answered their needs. Provision always came at just the right time – money, healing, or people with the skills needed to see a new project through. The present beauty of the campus is testament to their vision, willingness to learn, perseverance and downright hard work.

In 1994, Ken and Frieda left the home they had started, handing it over to Indian co-workers, and went into the nearby city of Dehra Dun to start a new work among high school students, simply because God was calling them onward. Leaving the home that they'd poured their lives into over so many years was not easy, but God had called and they chose to go. And so, the Doon Youth Centre was born; temporarily located in a large room above a bank in the centre of Dehra Dun, a city that is home to a large number of boarding schools. The Youth Centre has become a haven for many lonely, hurting young people – youth struggling with life issues but receiving little in the way of support from schools or, sadly, parents. The Youth Centre has become the one place where they can open their hearts, be truly heard, and be accepted (often for the first time). Ken teaches his (tailor-made for India) Life Skills curriculum in many schools, and does workshops for parents and teachers.

Everything Ken and Frieda have achieved, they have achieved by working together and by listening to and obeying, the voice of God. In the early days, while Ken was busy with the administration of the home and working on the farm and his many building projects, Frieda was equally busy as Principal and teacher in the school she'd started, writing songs and leading worship for the small church that was growing out of the home, all the while caring for their own growing family and for the children who'd come into their care. Since their move to Dehra Dun, Frieda has been able to pursue her love of music and develop her latent writing skills, producing two albums of her own songs, each with short books, giving the best possible understanding of the whole truth.

It has been wonderful to follow the progress of Ken and Frieda's children as they've grown up, who are presently scattered across the globe, each one going on with God… testifying to the practical life-style of serving that has been rooted deeply in them. In brief, I am delighted by my relationship with Ken and Frieda and their family and am proud to be able to count them among my friends. My life has been enriched through knowing them and, in a small way, walking the journey with them. I have no hesitation in commending them and this book to you.

Phil Leighton
September 7th 2006

* Phil Leighton, along with his wife Elizabeth and their children have been volunteers and supporters of the children's home for many years. Their faithful input to the children in the home, as well as to us personally, has been refreshing – often coming just when it was needed. Special thanks to Phil for his many trips to visit and revisit us; he is appreciated more than he can ever know.

Frieda McRae

Holy Spirit
Produced by Frieda McRae and Michael Sethi

It seems that I will never write a song again
For your Spirit falls upon me, I know not when
Your power overwhelms me
Humbles me within, I pray, Oh God
Put a new song on my lips again

From the power of Your love
And the life of Your Word
Filling me up and
Bowing me down before my God

Holy Spirit, Breath of Life
Breathe on me and give me life
Spirit come upon me in such a way
That I might know newness of day

Holy Spirit, Breath of Life
I fall before Your awesome light
Spirit come upon me
So that all I know
Will be from You alone

Just So Close
Produced by Frieda McRae and Michael Sethi

You came just so close to giving up all
You could almost see what is reality
Then you turned away from that light
You chose darkness, you chose night

You came just so close
To being held in His embrace
But you looked at the loss instead of the cross
You thought it was good
You thought it was right
But in choosing your way
You chose to die

Now I'm scared of the One
Who holds the key to life
For I know He upholds the cost of sacrifice
And I fear that my life
Has been lived without cost
Even that I have chosen, even that He bought

It took so long for me to know
Him who counts the cost and calls it love
To know Him who makes darkness turn to light
To know Him who turns mourning to joy
To know Him who wipes away every tear
To know Him who loves me as I am
And chooses me, to be His friend

Now I know, I understand
You came just so close
You could almost see
Then you turned away
You chose your way
You chose to die

All I Want
Produced by Christopher Hale and Peter Hicks

All I want is to know Christ
And to experience the power of His resurrection
All I want is to know Christ
And to experience His love

And to share in His sufferings
And become like Him in his death
In the hope that I might be
Raised from death to life

All I want is to gain the prize
For which Jesus won me to Himself
And for that I would run my whole life
To experience His love

Veil My Eyes
Produced by Christopher Hale and Peter Hicks

Lord my eyes are veiled to Thee
Still brillant radiance captures me
Lord veil my eyes to Your holiness
For I'm bound to your love mysteriously

Lord, like a child I see Your face
Like a child I feel Your embrace
Don't lift the veil Lord, awesome God
Till by grace I'm clothed with You above

Don't lift that veil Lord, lest I die
I know I need to be wholly sanctified
Let all creation announce your love
That unveils Jesus, who face to face will come

Rend Your Heart
Produced by Chris Hale and Peter Hicks

पवित्र, पवित्र, पवित्र है प्रभु
Holy, holy, holy Lord

Rend your heart before the Lord
Even now, rend your heart
Return to the Lord evening-morning
Return now, with all your heart

Rend your heart and not your clothes
Even now, declares the Lord
The day of the Lord is great and dreadful
The whole earth shakes, and the sky trembles

What a God whose boundless love
Spins the earth, ignites the sun
Can this God of hell and wrath
Heal the sick and make us laugh?
O Lord, you held children in your lap
All was sacrificed for every man

Jesus Said
Produced by Frieda McRae and Michael Sethi

Poor little child left all alone
Left in the cold without a coat
Without someone to keep you warm
Poor little child, we wish you weren't born!

We have a mother, she looks after us
We have our brothers they're a very fine bunch
We live together in a warm little house
And you are the child who will die untouched

Yes, poor little children you live far and near
We see you on the news
And on our street corner, too
Your world won't have you, we have the world
Our world wants us, in fact, we are the world!

We are the world, the voice that goes forth
We are the judges, a new truth we force
We are the ones to step in God's place
To create a utopia for the whole human race, oh!

Jesus said you are my family
You who hear God's word and do it
I have no mother and I have no brother
But them who love to follow God's Word
It is they who are my mother and my brother
It is they who are my family

यीशु ने कहा वह मेरा परिवार
जो वचन को सुनते और करते हैं।
मेरी न माँ, न है कोई भाई
सिर्फ़ वह जो खुदा को मानते हैं।
वही मेरी माँ, वही मेरा भाई,
वही है मेरा परिवार।

Touch the Feet
Produced by Christopher Hale and Peter Hicks

Touch the feet for you are made from dust
And you know that the One who walked in dirt
Has His throne on holy ground, so
Touch the feet

I touch the feet I feel the flesh of Him
Whose tears and blood are mixed
To become wine for me
Through His sweat I touch His feet

Touch the feet of the Christ
Wipe the stain from Him who died
Standing up unashamed
Stripped of pride it remains
To touch the feet

Lord, how can I come into Your presence now?
Lord, how can I
walk through gates of splendor now?
I by Your great mercy come into Your house
In reverence and adoration
I bow before You now

Enter In
Produced by Frieda McRae and Michael Sethi

Come to the threshold of His holiness,
Prostrate yourself on His love,
Open your arms to embrace His grace
Enter into the presence of God.

I do believe, I believe Christ made the way
I do believe, I believe in His blood
He is the Lamb, the Lamb of God slain
Slain for sin giving victory unto God

I do expect to see the promises
Fulfilled in my life my eyes will see
The faithfulness of His grace poured out on us
Who continue to trust and believe

I do expect, I expect Christ to lead me
I do expect, I expect His blood sets me free
He is the Lamb, the Lamb of God slain
Slain for me, so I can come before God

Enter in, enter in
The invitation's to all
Enter in, enter in
And live in the fullness of God

Enter into His throne room
Enter into His holiness
Enter into his love, his embrace

Enter into His presence
Enter into His fullness
Enter into the Heart of God

I Release you
Produced by Christopher Hale and Peter Hicks

I release your spirit, to soar the skies
I release your desires to meet your God on high
I release your dreams, to be fulfilled
I release you, I release you

If I could ever give your heart's desire
(now is the time)
If I could ever see your faith as truth
(now is the time)
If I could ever send you to paradise itself
(now is the time)
For you I would give up all
For you, now is the time.

Blessed is the name of the Lord
Who understands the times
Blessed is the work of the Lord
Whose very breath is life
Blessed is the promise of God
To give eternal life

Blessed is he who walks in hope
And gives up his life

Thanks Dad
Produced by Frieda McRae and Michael Sethi

Thank you for being good to me
For all the things I couldn't see
I know I didn't do the same
But Your sorrow became my gain

I thought I was the one who knew best
What was good for me
You said the choice was mine to make
I'd have to face that I am
Free to make my choices
Free to know and see

Everything before me, good and bad alike
Every choice I make
I make to state that truth of life
I cannot blame parents
any people or circumstance
It is God's gift in all of us - freedom!

I never asked You for wealth
Just wanted You to be proud of me
I never asked You to do so much
Just wanted all Your love
And that you gave me
Though hurt and pain dug deep
You always cared and waited patiently for me.

Sacrificial love, means so much to me
Sacrificial love, sets the captives free
Sacrificial love, a choice not just for me

With all my heart I thank you, God,
With all my heart I thank you, Dad,
With every breath and every step I make
I thank you Lord.
धन्यवाद

Satisfied
Produced by Frieda McRae and Michael Sethi

In me I find the need for You
My heart desires You
With aching heart and hungry spirit
I wait and watch for You

Even when renewed in spirit and in my soul
I only thirst and hunger more for You
It does not seem my search will end
To live closer to You
But in the morning when I rise
I am satisfied with You

In the cold while darkness reigns
I find that meeting Your embrace
Satisfies my soul
Though I long for Your power released
I am satisfied You reside in me
I am satisfied with You

I lie and rest in Your presence
My head upon Your breast
I hear Your heart beating my time
I am ever so satisfied
I am satisfied with You

Keep Me as Your Child
Produced by Frieda McRae

Lord, keep me as Your child
For I find that my heart calls out, Father!
My hair is growing white
While my eyes lose their sight
Still I find myself a child in Your embrace
Lord, keep me as your child

I wish to claim that age has left me wise
Each new day brings trials
That I find I've never tried
Though I'm old I still fall
And I find myself surrounded by empty walls

Finding there is no escape
From the evil we face
I give up and I call on Your name
Then again, as a child
I am found resting in Your embrace

Constant love, faithfulness
Timeless Father, relationship
Changeless One, hears my cry
Jesus, You're there with every sigh

Song writing has been a passion since my early teens. By the time I completed high school, my notebook boasted more than hundred teenybopper lyrics and tunes... luckily, the diary they were written in was lost. Recording and producing songs remained only a dream for many years. Another dream from childhood was to go to India and work with needy children. Both dreams were fulfilled; this project has connected the dreams together.

holy spirit	**Lead Vocal:** Frieda McRae **Accompanying lead vocals:** Sonu Kumar, Elizabeth Lal, Sheva McRae, Josie Kampa **Harmonies:** Michael Sethi, Frieda McRae, Christopher Hale **Children's voices:** Nishal, Noel, Niveh Eisenberg
just so close	
all i want	**Instruments:** **Sarod:** Peter Hicks **Acoustic Guitar:** Frieda McRae, Peter Hicks, Christopher Hale, Jurgen Eisenberg **Bass Guitar:** Hemendra Nath
veil my eyes	**Electric Guitar:** Ramesh J.K. **Violin and Mandolin:** Michael Sethi **Tabla and Dholak:** Ifftakear Alam
rend your heart	**Bansuri and Shehnai:** Sahabe Alam **Sarangi:** Vinod Kumar Mishra **Tanpura:** Christopher Hale, Sibte Hasan
jesus said	**Sitar:** Sibte Hassan All songs and lyrics by Frieda McRae
touch the feet	**Cover design:** Obed Tewes
enter in	**Recorded at:** Deepali Studio, Lucknow, U.P. India **Recording Engineer:** Sarojeet Kumar Ghosh **Sound Engineer:** Mike Williams with Peter Hicks
i release you	**English Vocals:** Studio Music Matters, Dehra Dun, U.A. with **Recording Engineer:** Rajeev Massey **Computer Graphic Engineer:** Shalom Lazarus, eMi^2, Mussoorie
thanks dad	**Illustrations:** Lindsay Kumar, Luke and Kirti Gilbert, Sanjeev Mehto, Nibha McRae, Sheva McRae, Frieda McRae
satisfied	**Music Video:** Jenni Nelson
keep me as your child	**Contact Frieda at:** frieda.mcrae@gmail.com www.friedamcrae.com